CRUSH YOUR FEARS

CRUSH YOUR FEARS

100 Powerful Promises to Overcome Anxiety

Daniel B Lancaster

LIGHTKEEPER BOOKS
NASHVILLE, TENNESSEE

For Ron and Joan Capps

CONTENTS

Preface xi

100 Powerful Promises Against Anxiety 1

Can You Help Me Help Others? 27
BONUS 29
Fear is a Liar 31
Books by the Author 55
About the Author 57

PREFACE

My prayer is this book will strengthen your walk with God. May you draw closer to Jesus every day and be filled with the Spirit. May you have a deep sense in your spirit that God loves you and will help you defeat any fear.

I have included several bonus gifts that I believe will be a blessing to you. The free *Crush Your Fears Bonus Pak* which includes:

40 Powerful Scripture Promises to Conquer Fear

40 Powerful Quotes to Crush Fear

40 Powerful Prayers for your War Room

All are suitable for framing. CLICK HERE to download your free *Crush Your Fears Bonus Pak.*

Read an excerpt from my bestselling book *Fear is a Liar.* God has blessed many through this book and I wanted to give you a chance to "try before you buy."

If you like this book, please leave a review. Your feedback will help other believers find this book easier and encourage me in my calling to write practical, powerful books to encourage, equip, and empower Christians throughout the world.

Blessings,

Daniel B Lancaster

CRUSH YOUR FEARS

Nashville, Tennessee — August 2019

100 POWERFUL PROMISES AGAINST ANXIETY

"No weapon that is fashioned against you shall succeed, and you shall confute every tongue that rises against you in judgment. This is the heritage of the servants of the Lord and their vindication from me," declares the Lord. Isaiah 54:17 (ESV)

◇

He has said to me, "My grace is sufficient for you, for power is perfected in weakness."
2 Corinthians 12:9 (NASB)

◇

Send me a sign of your favor.
Then those who hate me will be put to shame,
for you, O Lord, help and comfort me.
Psalm 86:17 (NLT)

◇

Do not fear, for I am with you;
Do not anxiously look about you, for I am your God.
I will strengthen you, surely I will help you,
Surely I will uphold you with My righteous right
hand. Isaiah 41:10 (NASB)

◇

If you are tired from carrying heavy burdens, come
to me and I will give you rest. Take the yoke I give
you. Put it on your shoulders and learn from me. I
am gentle and humble, and you will find rest. This
yoke is easy to bear, and this burden is light.
Matthew 11:28-30 (CEV)

◇

No temptation has overtaken you but such as is

common to man; and God is faithful, who will not
allow you to be tempted beyond what you are able,
but with the temptation will provide the way of
escape also, so that you will be able to endure it.
I Corinthians 10:13 (NASB)

◇

The Lord is a shelter for the oppressed,
a refuge in times of trouble. Psalm 9:9 (NLT)

◇

The Lord is my light and my salvation—whom shall
I fear? The Lord is the stronghold of my life—of
whom shall I be afraid? Psalm 27:1 (NIV)

◇

He will not fear bad news; his heart
is confident, trusting in the Lord.
His heart is assured; he will not fear.
In the end he will look in triumph on his foes.
Psalm 112:7-8 (HCSB)

◇

3

Anxiety in a man's heart weighs it down,
But a good word makes it glad. Proverbs 12:25 (NIV)

◇

The Lord is near the brokenhearted;
He saves those crushed in spirit.
Psalm 34:18 (HCSB)

◇

Now faith is the assurance of things hoped for, the
conviction of things not seen. Hebrews 11:1 (ESV)

◇

God is our refuge and strength,
always ready to help in times of trouble.
Psalm 46:1 (NLT)

◇

Five sparrows are sold for just two pennies, but God
doesn't forget a one of them. Even the hairs on your
head are counted. So, don't be afraid! You are worth
much more than many sparrows. Luke 12:6-7 (CEV)

◇

Cast your burden on the Lord, and He will sustain you; He will never allow the righteous to be shaken.
Psalm 55:22 (HCSB)

◇

When I am afraid, I put my trust in you.
Psalm 56:3 (NLT)

◇

He said, "Do not be afraid, for those who are with us are more than those who are with them." Then Elisha prayed and said, "O Lord, please open his eyes that he may see." So the Lord opened the eyes of the young man, and he saw, and behold, the mountain was full of horses and chariots of fire all around Elisha. 2 Kings 6:16-17 (ESV)

◇

Give up your sins—
even those you do in secret.
Then you won't be ashamed;
you will be confident
and fearless. Job 11:14-15 (CEV)

◇

Behold, God is my salvation,
I will trust and not be afraid;
For the Lord God is my strength and song,
And He has become my salvation.
Isaiah 12:2 (NASB)

◇

From the bottom of the pit,
I prayed to you, Lord.
I begged you to listen.
"Help!" I shouted. "Save me!"
You answered my prayer
and came when I was in need.
You told me, "Don't worry!"
You rescued me and saved my life.
Lamentations 3:55-58 (CEV)

◇

Greater than the roar of many waters—
the mighty breakers of the sea—
the Lord on high is majestic.
Psalm 93:4 (HCSB)

◇

If we truly love God,
our sins will be forgiven;
if we show him respect,
we will keep away from sin.
Proverbs 16:6 (CEV)

◇

He gives strength to the weary,
And to him who lacks might He increases power.
Isaiah 40:29 (NASB)

◇

Since therefore the children share in flesh and blood,
he himself likewise partook of the same things, that
through death he might destroy the one who has the
power of death, that is, the devil, and deliver all
those who through fear of death were subject to life-
long slavery. Hebrews 2:14-15 (ESV)

◇

Blessed be the God and Father of our Lord Jesus
Christ, the Father of mercies and God of all com-

fort, who comforts us in all our affliction so that we will be able to comfort those who are in any affliction with the comfort with which we ourselves are comforted by God. 2 Corinthians 1:3-4 (NASB)

◇

What then are we to say about these things? If God is for us, who is against us? Romans 8:31 (HCSB)

◇

I tell you not to worry about your life. Don't worry about having something to eat, drink, or wear. Isn't life more than food or clothing?
Matthew 6:25 (CEV)

◇

Then he said to them, "Go, eat of the fat, drink of the sweet, and send portions to him who has nothing prepared; for this day is holy to our Lord. Do not be grieved, for the joy of the Lord is your strength."
Nehemiah 8:10 (NIV)

◇

Jesus, overhearing what was being spoken, said to

the synagogue official, "Do not be afraid any longer,
only believe." Mark 5:36 (NIV)

◇

For the Lord your God is living among you.
He is a mighty savior.
He will take delight in you with gladness.
With his love, he will calm all your fears.
He will rejoice over you with joyful songs."
Zephaniah 3:17 (NLT)

◇

There is no fear in love; but perfect love casts out
fear, because fear involves punishment, and the one
who fears is not perfected in love.
1 John 4:18 (NASB)

◇

When doubts filled my mind, your comfort gave me
renewed hope and cheer. Psalm 94:19 (NLT)

◇

Since then we have a great high priest who has
passed through the heavens, Jesus, the Son of God,

let us hold fast our confession. For we do not have a high priest who is unable to sympathize with our weaknesses, but one who in every respect has been tempted as we are, yet without sin. Let us then with confidence draw near to the throne of grace, that we may receive mercy and find grace to help in time of need. Hebrews 4:14-16 (ESV)

◇

He got up and rebuked the wind and said to the sea, "Hush, be still." And the wind died down and it became perfectly calm. And He said to them, "Why are you afraid? Do you still have no faith?" Mark 4:39-40 (NIV)

◇

Keep your life free from love of money, and be content with what you have, for he has said, I will never leave you nor forsake you. So we can confidently say, The Lord is my helper; I will not fear; what can man do to me? Hebrews 13:5-6 (ESV)

◇

Be strong and courageous. Do not be afraid or terri-

fied because of them, for the Lord your God goes
with you; he will never leave you nor forsake you.
Deuteronomy 31:6 (NASB)

◇

The Lord is my strength and song,
And He has become my salvation;
This is my God, and I will praise Him;
My father's God, and I will extol Him.
Exodus 15:2 (NASB)

◇

The Lord is for me; I will not fear;
What can man do to me?
The Lord is for me among those who help me;
Therefore, I will look with satisfaction on those who
hate me. Psalm 118:6-7 (NIV)

◇

I will walk freely in an open place
because I seek Your precepts.
I will speak of Your decrees before
kings and not be ashamed.
I delight in Your commands, which I love.

I will lift up my hands to Your commands,
which I love and will meditate on Your statutes.
Psalm 119:45-48 (HCSB)

◇

When I saw him, I fell at his feet as if I were dead.
But he laid his right hand on me and said, "Don't be
afraid! I am the First and the Last."
Revelation 1:17 (NLT)

◇

So that He sets on high those who are lowly,
And those who mourn are lifted to safety.
Job 5:11 (NIV)

◇

I call to You from the ends of the earth
when my heart is without strength.
Lead me to a rock that is high above me...
Psalm 61:2 (HCSB)

◇

I would have despaired unless I had believed that I
would see the goodness of the Lord In the land

*of the living. Wait for the Lord; Be strong
and let your heart take courage;
Yes, wait for the Lord. Psalm 27:13-14 (NIV)*

◇

*We know that all things work together for the good
of those who love God: those who are called according to His purpose. Romans 8:28 (HCSB)*

◇

*Christ gives me the strength to face anything.
Philippians 4:13 (CEV)*

◇

*If you respect the Lord, you and your children have a
strong fortress and a life-giving fountain that keeps
you safe from deadly traps. Proverbs 14:26-27 (CEV)*

◇

*The Lord will fight for you, and you have only
to be silent. Exodus 14:14 (ESV)*

◇

That's why I take pleasure in my weaknesses, and in the insults, hardships, persecutions, and troubles that I suffer for Christ. For when I am weak, then I am strong. 2 Corinthians 12:10 (NASB)

◇

"For I know the plans I have for you," declares the Lord, "plans for welfare and not for evil, to give you a future and a hope." Jeremiah 29:11 (ESV)

◇

For the angel of the Lord is a guard; he surrounds and defends all who fear him. Psalm 34:7 (NLT)

◇

If we confess our sins, He is faithful and righteous to forgive us our sins and to cleanse us from all unrighteousness. 1 John 1:9 (NASB)

◇

Therefore, no condemnation now exists for those in Christ Jesus, because the Spirit's law of life in Christ Jesus has set you free from the law of sin and of death. Romans 8:1-2 (HCSB)

◇

Even when I go through the darkest valley, I fear no danger, for You are with me; Your rod and Your staff—they comfort me. Psalm 23:4 (HCSB)

◇

Do not be afraid of them; the Lord your God himself will fight for you. Deuteronomy 3:22 (NASB)

◇

Say to those who have an anxious heart, Be strong; fear not! Behold, your God will come with vengeance, with the recompense of God. He will come and save you. Isaiah 35:4 (ESV)

◇

But now, thus says the Lord, your Creator, O Jacob, And He who formed you, O Israel, "Do not fear, for I have redeemed you; I have called you by name; you are Mine!" Isaiah 43:1 (NIV)

◇

15

*No, despite all these things, overwhelming victory is
ours through Christ, who loved us.*
Romans 8:37 (NLT)

◇

*Do not fear those who kill the body but cannot kill
the soul. Rather fear him who can destroy both soul
and body in hell. Matthew 10:28 (CEV)*

◇

*Let the peace of Christ rule in your hearts, to which
indeed you were called in one body. And
be thankful. Colossians 3:15 (ESV)*

◇

*If you listen to me, you will be safe and
secure without fear of disaster.*
Proverbs 1:33 (CEV)

◇

*You keep him in perfect peace whose mind is stayed
on you, because he trusts in you. Isaiah 26:3 (ESV)*

◇

Therefore, we will not be afraid, though the earth trembles and the mountains topple into the depths of the seas, Psalm 46:2 (HCSB)

◇

For God has not given us a spirit of fear, but of power and of love and of a sound mind. 2 Timothy 1:7 (NASB)

◇

O may Your lovingkindness comfort me, According to Your word to Your servant. Psalm 119:76 (NIV)

◇

He who dwells in the shelter of the Most High will rest in the shadow of the Almighty. I will say of the Lord, He is my refuge and my fortress, my God, in whom I trust. Psalm 91:1-2 (NLT)

◇

My health may fail, and my spirit may grow weak, but God remains the strength of my heart; he is mine forever. Psalm 73:26 (NLT)

17

◇

*I lie down and sleep; I wake again because the
Lord sustains me. Psalm 3:5 (HCSB)*

◇

*The Lord God is my strength,
And He has made my feet like hinds' feet,
And makes me walk on my high places.
Habakkuk 3:19 (NASB)*

◇

*The fear of the Lord is the beginning of wisdom; all
who follow His instructions have good insight.
His praise endures forever. Psalm 111:10 (HCSB)*

◇

*Then, because you belong to Christ Jesus, God will
bless you with peace that no one can completely
understand. And this peace will control the way you
think and feel. Philippians 4:7 (CEV)*

◇

The Lord is my shepherd; there is nothing I lack.

He lets me lie down in green pastures;
He leads me beside quiet waters.
He renews my life; He leads me along the right paths
for His name's sake. Psalm 23:1-3 (HCSB)

◊

For you did not receive a spirit of slavery to fall back
into fear, but you received the Spirit of adoption, by
whom we cry out, "Abba, Father!"
Romans 8:15 (HCSB)

◊

Therefore, humble yourselves under the mighty hand
of God, that He may exalt you at the proper time,
casting all your anxiety on Him, because He
cares for you. 1 Peter 5:6-7 (NIV)

◊

Have I not commanded you? Be strong and coura-
geous! Do not tremble or be dismayed, for the Lord
your God is with you wherever you go.
Joshua 1:9 (NIV)

◊

Peace I leave with you; My peace I give to you; not as the world gives do I give to you. Do not let your heart be troubled, nor let it be fearful.
John 14:27 (NIV)

◇

I pray that God will take care of all your needs with the wonderful blessings that come from Christ Jesus!
Philippians 4:19 (CEV)

◇

The Lord works wonders and does great things.
Joel 2:21 (CEV)

◇

For the Lord your God is the one who goes with you, to fight for you against your enemies, to save you.
Deuteronomy 20:4 (NASB)

◇

I lift my eyes toward the mountains.
Where will my help come from?
My help comes from the Lord, the Maker of heaven and earth. Psalm 121:1-2 (HCSB)

◇

The Lord said to Paul one night in a vision, "Do not be afraid, but go on speaking and do not be silent, for I am with you, and no one will attack you to harm you, for I have many in this city who are my people." Acts 18:9-10 (ESV)

◇

Don't worry about anything but pray about everything. With thankful hearts offer up your prayers and requests to God. Philippians 4:6 (CEV)

◇

When you pass through the waters, I will be with you; and through the rivers, they shall not overwhelm you; when you walk through fire you shall not be burned, and the flame shall not consume you. Isaiah 43:2 (ESV)

◇

For I am the Lord your God, who upholds your right hand, Who says to you, "Do not fear, I will help you." Isaiah 41:13 (NASB)

21

◇

I will ask the Father, and He will give you another Helper, that He may be with you forever; that is the Spirit of truth, whom the world cannot receive, because it does not see Him or know Him, but you know Him because He abides with you and will be in you. John 14:16-17 (NIV)

◇

I prayed to the Lord, and he answered me. He freed me from all my fears. Psalm 34:4 (NLT)

◇

So do not worry about tomorrow; for tomorrow will care for itself. Each day has enough trouble of its own. Matthew 6:34 (NIV)

◇

*With all my heart
I praise the Lord,
and with all that I am
I praise his holy name!
With all my heart*

I praise the Lord!
I will never forget
how kind he has been.
Psalm 103:1-2 (CEV)

◇

With all your heart
you must trust the Lord
and not your own judgment.
Always let him lead you,
and he will clear the road
for you to follow.
Proverbs 3:5-6 (CEV)

◇

I am convinced that nothing can ever separate us
from God's love. Neither death nor life, neither
angels nor demons, neither our fears for today nor
our worries about tomorrow—not even the powers
of hell can separate us from God's love.
Romans 8:38 (NLT)

◇

Consider the ravens, for they neither sow nor reap;

*they have no storeroom nor barn, and yet God feeds
them; how much more valuable you are than the
birds! And which of you by worrying can add a sin-
gle hour to his life's span? If then you cannot do even
a very little thing, why do you worry about
other matters? Luke 12:24-26 (NIV)*

◇

*But let him ask in faith, with no doubting, for the
one who doubts is like a wave of the sea that is dri-
ven and tossed by the wind. For that person must
not suppose that he will receive anything from the
Lord; he is a double-minded man, unstable in all his
ways. James 1:6-8 (ESV)*

◇

*I love the Lord, because He hears
My voice and my supplications.
Because He has inclined His ear to me,
Therefore, I shall call upon Him as long as I live.
Psalm 116:1-2 (NIV)*

◇

Jesus said to his disciples, "Don't be worried! Have faith in God and have faith in me." John 14:1 (CEV)

◇

Finally, be strong in the Lord and in the strength of His might. Ephesians 6:10 (NASB)

◇

Don't be afraid of anyone! Everything that is hidden will be found out, and every secret will be known. Matthew 10:26 (CEV)

◇

Now may the God of hope fill you with all joy and peace as you believe in Him so that you may overflow with hope by the power of the Holy Spirit. Romans 15:13 (HCSB)

◇

These things I have spoken to you, so that in Me you may have peace. In the world you have tribulation, but take courage; I have overcome the world." John 16:33 (NIV)

◇

The fear of man brings a snare,
But he who trusts in the Lord will be exalted.
Proverbs 29:25 (NIV)

◇

Even if you should suffer for the sake of righteous-
ness, you are blessed. And do not fear their intimida-
tion, and do not be troubled...
1 Peter 3:14 (NASB)

◇

For we know that if the tent that is our earthly home
is destroyed, we have a building from God, a house
not made with hands, eternal in the heavens.
2 Corinthians 5:1 (ESV)

Can You Help Me Help Others?

BEFORE YOU GO, I'd like to say "thank you" again for buying this resource with 100 powerful promises to defeat anxiety and worry. I know you could have picked from dozens of books, but you chose this one. So, a big thanks for downloading this book and reading it all the way to the end.

Now I'd like to ask for a *small* favor. Could you please take a minute or two and leave a short review for this book? There is no greater way to thank me than this!

Think of it as a testimony to other believers about how this book helped you and could benefit them.

And if you loved it, then please let me know that too!

BONUS

Don't forget to download your free *Crush Your Fears Bonus Pak*!

I have included several bonus gifts that I believe will be a blessing to you. The free *Crush Your Fears Bonus Pak* which includes:

40 Powerful Scripture Promises to Conquer Fear

40 Powerful Quotes to Crush Fear

40 Powerful Prayers for your War Room

All are suitable for framing. CLICK HERE to download your free *Crush Your Fears Bonus Pak.*

Read an excerpt from my bestselling book *Fear is a Liar.* God has blessed many through this book and I wanted to give you a chance to "try before you buy."

FEAR IS A LIAR

INTRODUCTION

This is a simple book about how to overcome your fears and experience God's love more deeply.

Doesn't it seem like people used to live simpler, happier lives? Now, many of us are slowly turning into fearful, suspicious people. And fearful, suspicious people are often lonely people. We worry about being rejected by our friends, our loved ones dying, losing our jobs, and failing as parents. We worry about sexual predators, increased crime, the rise in severe weather events, and whether we will have enough money when we retire.

When you try to stop thinking about your fears, they only get stronger. Then, you try to ignore your fears, but that makes them bigger. What's a person to do?

As a missionary, I've faced all kinds of terrifying situations. I've been in earthquakes and hotel fires. I've been trailed by the secret police. Our family moved to a place where soldiers with machine guns guarded every major intersection in the capital city (You can imagine how terrifying it was just driving around). I also know firsthand about the fears that come when ovarian cancer takes your precious wife of thirty years.

I remember a time overseas when all the blood in my body settled in my legs. My wife and I had just learned a mother cobra and her babies decided to live in the flower bed where our children loved to play. A friend discovered the four-foot cobra when it raised its head and swayed back and forth.

Thankfully, he killed the venomous snake and her offspring while we were out of the country renewing our visas. I'll never forget how white my wife's face looked when she heard the news and how I held her arm to steady her.

Our family faced many fearful experiences while we ministered in a foreign land. We had to learn how to deal with our fears or be overwhelmed by them. Sometimes we failed mis-

> WE HAD TO LEARN HOW TO DEAL WITH OUR FEARS OR BE OVERWHELMED BY THEM.

erably in our fight against fear. Slowly though, we learned the steps in the LOVE Plan and saw more victories than defeats. I believe God will help you do the same.

Jesus said in the last days that fear would increase on the earth. Clearly, people struggle with worry and anxiety today more than ever.

> *And there will be signs in sun and moon and stars, and on the earth distress of nations in perplexity because of the roaring of the sea and the waves, people fainting with fear and with foreboding of what is coming on the world. For the powers of the heavens will be shaken. Luke 21:25–26 (ESV)*

In this book, you will learn a biblical plan to overcome whatever fear you may face. God hasn't given you a spirit of fear and wants you to defeat the flaming lying arrows of the evil one.

You will benefit along the way by developing a deeper walk with God and love for other people. You will also discover some good ways to do self-care. This book will teach you how to fill your love tank and not run on "almost empty" any longer.

This book will teach you how to:

- *Identify your root fears*

- *Understand why fears are so powerful*

- *Learn how Jesus dealt with fear*

- *Practice a four-step biblical plan to stop fear in its tracks*

- *Experience deeper love for God, others, and yourself*

At the end of this book, my prayer is that you can say:

> *I prayed to the Lord, and he answered me.*
> *He freed me from all my fears.*
> *Psalm 34:4 (NLT)*

Always remember, friend, fear is a liar. I've shared the truth of these principles throughout the world, and they have helped many overcome their fears. I believe God will do the same in your life. As you practice the LOVE Plan, you will hear the Holy Spirit more clearly, and your fears will lose their power over your mind, heart, soul, and spirit.

And it gets even better: You will be able to share these simple truths with your friends and family and see their lives transformed as well. Just imagine the gift you will give your children of knowing how to let perfect love cast out their fears (See 1 John 4:18).

As we journey through this book together, you will learn a new way of living, conquer your fears, and become more like Jesus. God wants that. You want that. I want that. So, let's get started.

In the next chapter, we'll travel back to the first fear recorded in the Bible.

CHAPTER 1 – WHY WE WORRY

WORRY OFTEN GIVES A SMALL THING A BIG SHADOW.

– SWEDISH PROVERB

Fears are tricky, little devils.

They are like the little weeds in your yard or gar-den—you hardly give them a thought. But, the longer you wait to remove them, the more weeds they produce. If you wait too long, they choke out the good plants and everything looks ... well ... just ugly.

When you feel like the whole world is ugly, it is a sign you have a fear problem. When your relation-ships feel ugly, it is a sign you have a fear problem. When your God-ordained future seems ugly, it is a sign you have a fear problem.

The first step in overcoming fears is to understand why and where they originally entered the world. That's what we will explore in this chapter. I will show you how Satan first enslaved humanity with fear. It turns out fear and worry have filled people's hearts and minds for an awfully long time.

Along the way, you will discover how the hater tries to manipulate your mind and heart and turn the good from God in your life into evil. You will realize the hater wants you to over analyze everything in your life

> FEAR AND WORRY HAVE FILLED PEOPLE'S HEARTS AND MINDS FOR AN AWFULLY LONG TIME.

and paralyze you with fear. This gives Satan even more time to fill your mind with untruths.

Just being aware of his evil schemes will help you walk on the narrow Path of Love instead of wandering on the broad Path of Fear. Understanding why you have fears is an important step to becoming more confident as you fight them.

My prayer is you will once again see the beauty of God brighten every corner of your life. To do that, we will go back to a garden called Eden.

THE NARROW PATH OF LOVE

Imagine working and playing in the Garden of Eden before Adam and Eve sinned. Everything they did had so much meaning.

Adam and Eve looked forward to the cool of the day. God would come down, and they shared their hearts with Him. He shared His heart with them too. It's easy to imagine what their conversations were like. Love. Love. Love.

Eve shared with God how proud she was of Adam. He was so smart; he had named all the animals! Adam smiled sheepishly and said it was nothing. Eve made him feel ten feet tall.

Adam shared with Eve how lonely life was before she came. Adam thanked God every evening for giving him such an incredible gift. Eve probably blushed and told Adam to stop making such a big deal out of her.

God praised Adam for his heart to be a rock for Eve and someone she could always count on. They noticed a tear in God's eye when He praised Adam for sacrificing for his wife.

God praised Eve for how beautiful she was making everything in the garden and for her creativity. Eve felt so honored and cherished and celebrated.

Oh, the joy to walk on the Path of Love with no fear!

Adam and Eve may have talked with God about having children. They had seen the animals give birth and wondered if humans could too. Or would God make their children as He had made them? Eve looked forward to a happy family that would make the world an even better place.

Adam asked God what had caused him to feel different inside when he climbed too high in a tree.

God explained He had put an emotion in Adam and Eve that told them when they were in danger. He had given them this feeling because He loved them and wanted them to be safe.

Just being close to God filled them with love and confidence. Walking with Him made them feel incredibly strong and wise. God answered every question about their world.

They laughed. They dreamed. They couldn't wait for each day to arrive.

THE BROAD PATH OF FEAR

But everything changed one day. Adam and Eve stopped walking on the narrow Path of Love. Genesis 3 tells about the painful entry of sin and fear into our world.

Now the serpent was more cunning than any beast
of the field which the LORD God had made. And
he said to the woman, "Has God indeed said, 'You
shall not eat of every tree of the garden'?"
Genesis 3:1 (NKJV)

Satan lures Eve down the Path of Fear by questioning God's command. The Great Manipulator, Satan, takes something good that God has said and makes it sound wrong or petty. He fills her mind with lies.

If you have ever known a self-centered person, you know the drill. Start by getting your target to reconsider a small action or decision. Cause them to doubt their instincts and trust you have their best interests in mind. But it's all a scam. They're luring you into their trap. This is exactly what Satan did in the garden.

Now Eve has started down the Path of Fear, thinking Satan's thoughts, and she doesn't even realize it. Satan has already deceived a third of the angels of heaven into following him. Eve has zero experience dealing with

> SATAN LURES EVE DOWN THE PATH OF FEAR BY QUESTIONING GOD'S COMMAND.

manipulation and deception. There's no way she's going to win.

> *And the woman said to the serpent, "We may eat the fruit of the trees of the garden; but of the fruit of the tree which is in the midst of the garden, God has said, 'You shall not eat it, nor shall you touch it, lest you die.' " Genesis 3:2–3 (NKJV)*

Talking with Satan is never a good idea, but that's exactly what Eve did. Satan is the Father of Lies and doesn't play fair. Even though Eve simply tells Satan what God commanded, she is still speaking with the enemy of her soul. Even Michael, the archangel, knew better than talk to Satan without God's help (Jude 9).

> *Then the serpent said to the woman, "You will not surely die. For God knows that in the day you eat of it your eyes will be opened, and you will be like God, knowing good and evil." Genesis 3:4–5 (NKJV)*

Now that Eve is thinking the way Satan wants her to, he openly questions God's goodness. Satan wants Eve to believe God doesn't have her best interest in mind. God created Eve as a helpmeet; her deep desire is to work with Adam to create a beautiful world.

Meanwhile, Satan tells her she is missing out. God is holding out on her and her husband. She wonders if God hasn't been telling the whole truth when she and Adam talked with Him in the cool of the day. Was God hiding something? Maybe He hasn't been meeting her needs as well as she thought He was. Satan has fueled a fire of suspicion in her mind and heart. Can she even trust God?

> *So when the woman saw that the tree was good for food, that it was pleasant to the eyes, and a tree desirable to make one wise, she took of its fruit and ate. She also gave to her husband with her, and he ate. Genesis 3:6 (NKJV)*

Eve relies on her own judgment instead of God's will and God's Word. The fruit looked good. The fruit looked beautiful. The fruit made one wise like God. It's all good.

She takes a bite of the fruit, and nothing happens immediately. So, she gives it to Adam. She probably felt like she had made the best decision in the world, and to show her husband how much she loved him, she shared it with him. Just think how they could help their kids if they were wise like God!

Then the eyes of both of them were opened, and they

*knew that they were naked; and they sewed fig
leaves together and made themselves coverings.*
Genesis 3:7 (NKJV)

Enter the first fear: shame. Disobedience opened
their eyes and closed their hearts. Adam and Eve saw
their nakedness and felt shame. They responded by
sewing fig leaves together, trying to hide their shame.

Satan knew the more shame Adam and Eve felt, the
more fears they would believe. They soon found that
one feeling of unworthiness in the heart can easily
create ten fears in the mind.

It's easy to imagine Eve
crying and apologizing to
Adam for what had hap-
pened. Her wrong think-
ing had created
overwhelming suffering

THE GARDEN OF
EDEN HAD TURNED
INTO THE GARDEN
OF FEAR.

for her and her husband. Eve thought she was doing
something good.

But everything changed to bad ... extremely bad.

The young couple looked at each other with different

eyes. Their feelings of love appeared fake compared to before. Shame and fear were clouding their vision.

The fear emotion they had experienced when climbing too high in a tree had been short-lived. It disappeared after the danger passed. Now they felt fear all the time. For the first time since God created them, Adam and Eve were suspicious of each other.

The Garden of Eden had turned into the Garden of Fear.

> *And they heard the sound of the LORD God walking in the garden in the cool of the day, and Adam and his wife hid themselves from the presence of the LORD God among the trees of the garden.*
> *Genesis 3:8 (NKJV)*

Enter the second fear: guilt. Before Adam and Eve ate the fruit, fear had kept them safe—kept them from danger. But now they felt suspicious and ashamed. Now they hid because they feared God's wrath for their sin.

Terror and trauma replaced the joy of hearing God's footsteps, coming for His evening walk with them.

Adam and Eve had felt peace and security in the

Garden of Eden. Now, negative thoughts filled their minds and made them feel hopeless. Their minds raced with bad pictures of the future and regrets from the past.

Eve couldn't stop her mind from thinking of what had happened and what she could do to help them stop feeling bad. She hid from God among the trees with Adam.

Feelings of loneliness, shame, and guilt rose from her heart into her mind, and she felt paralyzed by fear.

> *Then the LORD God called to Adam and said to him, "Where are you?" So he said, "I heard Your voice in the garden, and I was afraid because I was naked; and I hid myself." Genesis 3:9–10 (NKJV)*

If you have ever had a close friendship that ended badly, you know how Adam felt at this point. Before the fall, he walked and talked with God. He felt deeply loved and returned love with no fear. He was free to be creative and found life fulfilling.

But after the Hater deceived his wife, Adam was overwhelmed with unexpected feelings of shame and guilt. He felt afraid of God—the Lover of his soul!

We experience these same feelings when we fear. Deep inside, we say, "I am afraid; I am vulnerable, and I want to hide myself."

Life can feel hopeless with no plan to overcome constant fear.

> *And He said, "Who told you that you were naked? Have you eaten from the tree of which I commanded you that you should not eat?"*
>
> *Then the man said, "The woman whom You gave to be with me, she gave me of the tree, and I ate."*
> Genesis 3:11–12 (NKJV)

Enter the final two fears: blame and rejection.

Adam blames God for what happened, saying, "The woman whom you gave to be with me." Instead of taking responsibility for what happened, Adam points an accusing finger at God.

> LIFE CAN FEEL HOPELESS WITH NO PLAN TO OVERCOME CONSTANT FEAR.

Adam also rejects Eve. He had celebrated her; now, he criticizes her. He had rejoiced in God's gift; now, he rejects her. Why? Hurting people hurt people.

Imagine for a moment the pain of rejection that shot through Eve's heart when she heard those words.

Imagine the fiendish glee in Satan's darkened heart when he saw the tears in Eve's eyes.

Eve wondered where her rock had gone. She felt forsaken. Pictures of feeling distant from Adam the rest of their lives flooded her mind.

And the LORD God said to the woman, "What is this you have done?" The woman said, "The serpent deceived me, and I ate." Genesis 3:13 (NKJV)

Adam blamed Eve for what happened. Now Eve blames the serpent.

Her response is short. She probably thinks "less is more." But that approach doesn't work with her Creator. God knows her heart and mind better than she knows them herself.

The Blame Game started in the Garden of Eden and has never stopped. Sadly, blame has just grown more sophisticated through the ages.

- I know it was wrong, but you made me....

- I had a rough childhood, and that's the reason I....

- They deceived me, so I had to....

- I would have a better life if our leaders would....

The Blame Game is all about pointing at others, so no one points at you first.

So [God] drove out the man; and He placed cherubim at the east of the garden of Eden, and a flaming sword which turned every way, to guard the way to the tree of life. Genesis 3:24 (NKJV)

Can you imagine Adam and Eve leaving the garden, hiding their faces in shame? Instead of relying on God's love and wisdom, they blamed God, Satan, and each other for what happened.

Clothes made from the furs of innocent animals cover their bodies, but not their overwhelming sense of guilt. God removes them from the garden as an act of love, but they don't see it that way. They feel rejected and cast away.

> INSTEAD OF RELYING ON GOD'S LOVE AND WISDOM, THEY BLAMED GOD, SATAN, AND EACH OTHER FOR WHAT HAPPENED.

Adam's loneliness is a thousand times worse than his life before Eve. Eve is still Adam's help meet and wondering how she can help him get rid of these terrible feelings and get them to a better place emotionally.

Both imagine an uncertain future. They no longer feel safe. They feel insecure. Their minds whirl with questions and possible solutions:

- What will we do the next time we see Satan?

- Will God ever talk to us again?

- What will our sin and fears do to our children?

- Will we ever feel close to each other and God again?

- Will our marriage weather this storm?

In the Garden of Eden, every day was better than the day before, filled with new discoveries and adventures. Now, they believe every day will be worse and filled with difficult problems.

They had depended on God's life-giving wisdom for everything before their sin. Now, they feel mired in negative thinking and dark fears. They began to trust in the creation and not the Creator, and now they are in trouble.

Adam and Eve started walking on the Path of Fear and would continue until the day they died.

WHICH PATH ARE YOU ON?

Every person since Adam and Eve starts their journey through life on the Path of Fear. Some people stay on the path forever.

We are people of flesh and blood. That is why Jesus became one of us. He died to destroy the devil, who had power over death. But he also died to rescue all of us who live each day in fear of dying.
Hebrews 2:14–15 (CEV)

Living apart from God, we build up a huge amount of guilt, rejection, shame, and blame in our hearts and minds. If we don't deal with these issues, we influence the hearts and minds of our children and others with fear as well.

When you walk the Path of Fear, you believe God is not with you. So you resort to relying on your own thinking, efforts, and plans. Overcoming your fears is impossible because God is absent, and Satan's work is so strong. You believe everyone is a con.

You forget you are the one choosing what you believe. You are building your own Path of Fear.

When you walk the Path of Love, God is there. His strength, wisdom, and mercy cover you. Walking on the Path of Love strengthens your intimacy with God and makes defeating fears so much easier.

Satan cowers in the presence of Almighty God.

Believers who walk the Path of Love have painful memories, too. They see how their neediness has caused them to drift to the dark side sometimes. The main difference is they repent, return to Jesus, and ask Him to heal their past.

So, how do you walk on the Path of Love?

Some believers teach the answer to the fear problem is to think differently. Think positive thoughts. Don't be so negative. But thinking differently is only half the answer.

Satan has been tempting people with fear since the beginning—for thousands of years. Countless fears. Billions and billions of customers served.

Friend, I care about you enough to tell you the truth.

You don't stand a chance if you are trying to defeat your fears by controlling your negative thoughts. Satan knows too many ways to trip you up. He's been practicing a long time. In comparison, you just started.

If controlling thoughts was the way to defeat fear, Buddhists would be the healthiest, happiest people in the world. But Buddhist countries rank among the poorest and most corrupt. The Buddhist country we lived in for twelve years as missionaries was overcome with fear.

Hmm. Sounds like Satan's rule on the earth—whole countries walking the Path of Fear.

Beautiful people. Bad solution.

Trying to figure out how to control your negative thinking won't solve your fear problem. Some of the

FEAR IS A HEAD AND A HEART PROBLEM.

smartest people I know struggle with fear the most. Using this approach alone only makes your fears worse.

Why?

Because fear is a head and heart problem.

The answer is a different way of living, not just a different way of thinking. We need a way of living that helps us believe the best is yet to come. Not the other way around.

Find out more about *Fear is a Liar* HERE.

MORE FROM THIS AUTHOR

#1 Best Sellers

on

This series on powerful prayer, heart-felt worship, and intimacy with Christ will help strengthen your "War Room" and give you a battle plan for prayer.

Visit go.lightkeeperbooks.com/battleplan to learn more.

ABOUT THE AUTHOR

Daniel B Lancaster (PhD) enjoys training others to become passionate followers of Christ. He has planted two churches in America and trained over 5,000 people in Southeast Asia as a strategy coordinator with the *International Mission Board*. He served as Assistant Vice-President for University Ministries at *Union University* and currently is a international missionary with *Cornerstone International*. He has four grown children and a delightful grandson.

Dr. Dan is available for speaking and training events.

Contact him at dan@lightkeeperbooks.com to arrange a meeting for your group.